Carb Cycling

The 7-Day Carb Cycle Transformation – Carb Cycling Diet, Carb Cycling Recipes, Carb Cycling Meal Plans

© **Copyright 2016 - All rights reserved.**

Table of Contents

Introduction

If you are planning to go on a diet plan or have heard about most of the diet plans in the market, you would know that most diet plans talk about reducing carbohydrates in the diet. In fact, some diet plans completely eliminate the inclusion of any carbohydrate-rich food in the daily diet plan. It would not be wrong to state that carbohydrates are considered the enemy of weight loss and healthy living.

Contrary to popular belief, none of the macronutrients are bad for the body and carbohydrates are no exception to this rule. Just like any other macronutrient, carbohydrates can also be tailored for the individual in such a manner that they benefit the overall health of the individual. Cycling carbohydrates is one of the ways in which individuals can optimize their carbohydrate intake. This process is popularly known as Carb Cycling.

Carb Cycling Defined

Carb Cycling is a unique dietary approach in which the individual alternates carbohydrate intake on a weekly, daily or monthly basis. This approach can help in more than one way. First, it aids in weight loss. Secondly and more importantly, it allows the body to maintain physical performance even though the body is restricted by a diet regime. Moreover, it also prevents the body from hitting a plateau.

The most common approach that is followed by people is to alternate their carbohydrate intake on a daily basis.

However, you may also alternate carbohydrate intake for longer periods of time. The objective of following this regime is that the body must get its required dose of carbohydrates as and when the body requires it. On the other hand, the carbs must be excluded from the diet whenever they are not needed. This will help the body burn the carbohydrates for energy and not store anything, adding to weight gain.

The carb intake of the body can be programmed for individual preferences based on a lot of factors. Some of these factors include:

- Body Composition Goals
  A low-carb day is recommended when the body is on a diet. On the other hand, when the body is in performance phase or is training, the body needs carbs and a high carb day is recommended.

- Training and Rest Days
  The amount of carbohydrates that a body needs largely depends on the requirements of the body, which is in turn dependent on the day. For instance, if you are on a rest day, then your body doesn't need carbs and a low carb day would do. However, when you are on a training day, then your body requires energy for which carbs are required. Therefore, a high carb day will be most appropriate.

- Planning Re-feeds

If you have had a prolonged diet period, then you can go on several days of high carb diet. This period will act as a "re-feed".

- Energy-Intensive Events
  For people whose jobs require energy-intensive tasks, a high carb day for the event is recommended. This is particularly the case for athletes and people who participate in sports events and competitions.

- Training Type
  The carb intake and diet also needs to be in tandem with the exercise routine that you are following. In other words, if an individual is following very intensive and rigorous workout regimen, then he or she obviously requires more carbs than usual. The diet plan must accordingly adjust the extra carbs that the body requires.

- Levels of Body Fat
  As an individual progresses with his or her weight loss regime, he or she also needs to accommodate to the changing body fat levels of the individual. For instance, if the body of the individual is becoming leaner, then the high carb days must automatically increase in number.

Typically, an ideal carb cycling diet must include three low carb days, two medium carb days and two high carb days. Although, the protein constituent of the diet must remain unchanged throughout the week, the amount of fat included in the diet can vary on the basis of the amount of carbohydrates allowed. In other words, a high carb day will have low fat percentage. On the other hand, a low carb day will have high fat percentage. This carb cycling diet is an advanced strategy for diet planning.

The rest of the book will cover different facets of carb cycling, focusing on how carb cycling can benefit your health. Weight loss is one of the fundamental benefits of carb cycling. While your trainer will help you figure out a training regime for yourself, this book shall help you create a diet plan of your choice. This book includes many delectable recipes that you can include in your menu for a delicious and healthy plan. Besides this, the book also offers many tips and daily advice that you can include in your lifestyle.

Chapter 1: Origin of Carb Cycling

There was a time in the 1970s and 1980s called the 'high-carb mania'. Most of the popular diets of that time encouraged the intake of large amounts of carbohydrates. However, this perception changed drastically in the 1990s and an exact opposite became popular. The diets of the 1990s, and later, concentrated on reducing the carbohydrate in the diet, giving rise to the 'low-carb mania'.

With that said, people are still unclear about how the carbs are used up in the human body. More precisely, the contribution of carb amounts to any weight loss program needs to be understood. Without any understatement, it can be said that your carb intake can be the game changer in your weight loss program and be responsible for weight loss. On the other hand, it might just be the macronutrient that can destroy your plan completely.

Today, the scenario has changed and there are a plethora of resources available for people to study and know what their bodies are going through, with and without a weight loss regime. Despite this availability of resources, people are still facing weight issues so much so that obesity is one of the most common problems faced by the world today. This brings us to question as to why the scenario is deteriorating.

After much contemplation, experts have stated that the reason behind the increasing problem of obesity is that none of the existing fitness systems understands the functioning of the human body. Most of the existing dietary approaches end up lowering the body's metabolism. As a result, the body loses all its energy and motivation to lose weight, putting the weight loss program on a complete halt. Evidently, putting the body on a constant amount of carbohydrates cannot solve the issues and you'll need to vary the carbs in your diet to keep the ball rolling as far as weight loss is concerned.

Franco Carlotto created carb cycle regiment in the 1990s, in his attempt to prepare for the Mr. World Fitness Title. In the process, he also helped millions of people around the world in maintaining a lean and healthy body. The main objective of this dietary approach was to help people achieve not just their long-term weight loss goals, but to reach both the short-term and long-term milestones in time.

This technique has been developed from the analysis of how our ancestors ate and depleted their carb storage to maintain a healthy body. Although, the times have changed, the human body and the way it functions remains the same. Therefore, the solution to weight loss issues also remains the same in the 21st century. We have to understand and manipulate our own carb storage system to get the weight loss results we expect.

The carb cycle approach requires an individual to alternate high carb and low carb cycles on a daily basis, regulating the natural storage system of the body in such a way that the body doesn't store anything and burns more than what is expected on a daily and weekly basis. The low carb days deplete the body of its carbohydrates. However, the high carb days replenish the carb reserves. In this way, the body doesn't get exhausted of its energy and resources at any time. On a personal level, you don't have to give up on all your carbohydrate-rich foods altogether. You can just vary them on the basis of the day of the cycle and still reach your weight loss milestones.

Most practitioners of carb cycling recommend a basic carb cycling for beginners giving them a slow start and introduction to the world of dietary approaches. One of the best things about this dietary approach is that it doesn't restrict the individual to a point where he or she will start cheating on the diet. Therefore, the guilt that most people feel from not being able to follow the regime properly and losing the motivation doesn't have much of an effect on people following a carb cycling approach.

Any carb cycling approach is not just a dietary plan, but it is a complete way of life. It is a comprehensive fitness guide for an individual to follow through out their lives. The scope for adjustment in the carb cycling approach allows people to alter it on the basis of the changing needs of their body. Therefore, they can carry on with this fitness regime regardless of the age and fitness levels they reach. The benefits of this approach have been discussed in detail, in the following chapter. Although, carb cycling is a relatively new approach to dieting, its popularity speaks volumes about its effectiveness for people across ages and gender.

Chapter 2: What Can Carb Cycling Do For You?

Before dwelling into the benefits of carb cycling, let us first discuss the science behind carb cycling and how it works for you. Fundamentally, the concept of carb cycling uses the biological mechanism behind manipulation of carbohydrates in the human body. The ultimate aim of this dietary approach is to predict the carbohydrate needs of the body on a given day and provide it with the same. For instance, if you have a high training session planned for the day, then you will be given a high carb diet to keep your body active and energized to survive the training session.

Apart from fueling the body with energy, a high carb day also replenishes glycogen. This prevents excessive breakdown of the muscles and improves the body's performance. Lastly, giving high-carb diet to an individual in a planned and strategic manner can help the individual regulate the appetite regulating hormones like ghrelin and leptin, which in turn helps controls body weight.

On the other hand, when the body is forced into a low-carb diet on a 'low-carb' day, the body has to process the required energy from the fats supplied to or stored within the body. Therefore, during this phase, the body is switched to a fat-based energy system. It does not only improve the body's ability to use its fat reserve as body fuel, but it also improves the metabolic flexibility of the body.

Another important aspect of the low-carb day is that it manipulates the insulin levels of the body. Insulin is considered a marker that indicates how healthy or unhealthy a body is. When carbs are targeted around workouts and energy-intensive days, the insulin sensitivity of the body is expected to improve. From another viewpoint, the increased insulin sensitivity maximizes carbohydrate benefits for the body.

All in all, it can be stated that the carb cycling approach helps the body learn how to use fat as a source of energy generation, allowing it to burn more fats than usual. Therefore, theoretically, it reduces the fat reserve of the body, in due course of time, bringing the weight down considerably, apart from a range of other benefits that this dietary approach has for the human body.

Carb Cycling for Losing Weight

One of the most profound benefits of the carb cycling approach is weight loss. Cycling carbohydrates and giving the human body doses of carbs as and when the body requires it allows you to provide the body the benefits of a low-carb diet without depleting all the resources of the body and limiting energy. The primary objective of any weight loss program is to maintain a calorie deficiency.

When the body has less energy generated than what it needs for the day, it will automatically start burning its fat reserve for energy. However, this process, in order to show noticeable results, will require prolonged periods of following a calorie deficit approach. However, when the calorie deficit approach is implemented along with carb cycling, you can see better and quicker results. With that said, this combination can be rather complex and beginners may face issues in implementing it to its full capacity, at first.

It is because of these complexity issues that we recommend you to read this book and implement carb cycling for weight loss in a manner that can benefit you optimally and maximally. Most people who have used carb cycling believe that the best thing about this approach is the flexibility that it offers the users. You can adhere to the dietary approach without having to restrict your body beyond what you can afford. Regardless of the number of days you cycle low-carbs and high carbs, be sure to maintain a healthy protein intake. The carb cycling approach doesn't manipulate the protein content of your diet plan and it can essentially be constant on all days of the week.

Sports Performance and Muscle Growth for Carb Cyclers

The fact that carb cycling encourages people to increase their carbohydrate intake during training sessions helps increases the body energy of the individual during the concerned time. Consequently, a higher performance can be expected. There are several studies that indicate that carb cycling enhances the ability to build muscle, as well. This benefit is attributed to the fact that carbs can facilitate glycogen replenishment, nutrient delivery and recovery of muscle tears during workouts.

Reducing the carbs intake during workouts can increase muscle wear-tear and healing is considerably delayed. Some experts also indicate that carbs cycling can also create muscle growth. However, there is no scientific proof to attest to this fact. With that said, there are no two ways about the fact that carb cycling improves performance and facilitates recovery. In order to validate facts about the relationship between carb cycling and muscle growth/gain additional research is needed.

Additional Benefits of Carb Cycling

Apart from the traditional benefits of carb cycling, which are also provided by most dietary approaches, even though in reduced intensity and degree, carb cycling also provides some unique benefits to the body and overall health of the individual. None of the other diet programs contribute to human health in ways that this approach is capable of.

The fact that carb cycling allows the individual to go on alternate high and low carb days provides his or her body the benefits of both of these diet regimes, without the side-effects of either. While the low carb days improve insulin sensitivity, enhance metabolic activity and increase fat burning in the body, the high carb days bring the hormone levels in control and manipulate the appetite-generating hormones in such a manner that they can facilitate weight loss.

The combined benefits of these two diet plans allow sustained and long-term weight loss; the benefits of which can be obtained for much longer periods of time. While most weight loss plans benefit an individual for the first couple of weeks and fail with time, carb cycling can fit into the lifestyle of an individual no matter the age and health of the individual.

Chapter 3: Carb Cycling and Weight Loss

As we mentioned previously, one of the most popular and effective ways in which carb cycling can help you, is for losing weight. However, before you plan your carb cycling diet, there are a few things that you need to know. If you have ever had the opportunity to read about the different dietary approaches available, you would have come across carb cycling as one approach that gives you the benefits of different diets without inflicting any side effects on your body.

Some of the ill effects of other dietary approaches include increased cravings, reduced performance, diminishing metabolism and inability to concentrate on other day-to-day activities. The odd high carb days of the carb cycling plan help you gain your energy back and keep the body's energy and metabolism on track. This chapter elaborates on a few facets of the carb cycling weight loss program that you must be acquainted with before making a plan.

Position Training Sessions On High Carb Days

As a rule, you must always place training sessions on days that you have earmarked as high-carb. This can be treated as the formula for best results as far as carb cycling is concerned. If you are not sure as to which days are most intensive on the training, you can mark days on which you perform full-body workout or leg exercises. All of these days need require extreme energy unless you want to tear your body apart and exhaust yourself

Therefore, if you are still wondering why you need to take a carb-rich diet on these days, then the answer is as simple as this: your body needs carbs the most during physical activity. Having a rich meal before starting a workout session will refuel your body and prepare it for the physical stress. Moreover, it will also motivate your body to work harder and complete the workout as planned. Depleting your body of energy will keep your body from working hard and the workout regime will not yield the results that you expect it to give you.

In addition, a high carb meal after the workout will facilitate repair of the muscle damage done during the workout, in addition to saturating carbohydrate storage for the muscles. If you workout on all days and are unsure as to when you must plan your high carb days, you can earmark the workout sessions that are most rigorous. You should have the best carb diets on days you work the hardest.

An important facet of using high carb days on high training days is that the higher intake of carbohydrates will be consumed on these days and there is a much lower chance that this food will be stored in the body as fat. In order to succeed with this plan, you will also need to time your training days and high carb days appropriately during the course of the week.

Be Prepared For Water Weight Gain

Before you start with your carb cycling program, you must know that you will most likely experience water weight gain, particularly when you are on a high carb day. In fact, you can expect to gain 4 grams of water weight for every gram of carbohydrate that you consume. Therefore, if you are consuming about 300-400 grams of carbohydrates on a typical high carb day, you can imagine the amount of water you are storing for this carbohydrate.

This effect is all the more amplified for people who have a lean build for the simple reason that it is easier to notice any weight gain on them. However, be that as it may, this should not be a cause of worry for you. Since this gain is not adding any fat to your body, it is not an alarm and is just a part of the normal process. You will shed this weight as soon as you go back to a low carb day or a medium carb day.

Some people take any weight gain during the plan extremely seriously and this has a direct impact on their psychological makeup. How they look in the mirror is really important to them to maintain a healthy psychological state. For such people, carb cycling can be tough to implement and follow. If you fall under this category, you must either be prepared for this ill effect of this plan or do away with the idea of carb cycling altogether. I encourage you to stick with it and see how it works for you over time.

Choose Your Carbs Wisely

Food selection is one of the most critical facets of any weight loss program and given the variety of different carbohydrates available, you can have a tough time making selections. It is safest to think about glucose while making carbohydrate source selections. Sources of carbohydrates, simple or complex, that can directly breakdown into glucose are recommended. However, it is important to mention here that simple sources of glucose are best taken around workout sessions as they can be immediately absorbed in the body for instant energy, keeping the energy meter of the body on high.

Now that we have told you about the sources you must take, a word on the sources that you must completely avoid is equally vital. The one source that you must not include in your diet at any cost is fructose. Foods like a high-fructose corn syrup do not behave in the human body in the same manner as glucose. Therefore, it shall not benefit your body in the way that glucose is expected to, making this an inappropriate carb to consume. In fact, adding fructose-rich foods to your diet, even when on a high carb day, can cause fat storage in the body for the simple reason that fructose doesn't get absorbed in the muscles easily.

Reduce Fats When On High Carbs

The idea behind carb cycling is to keep the proteins constant while balancing the carbs and fats on high and low carb days. For instance, if you are on a high carb day, you will need to reduce the fat content of your food. On the other hand, if you are on a low carb day, the fat inclusion in your food must be accordingly higher. Evidently, the number of calories you consume on a high carb day will be higher than usual, but if you further lower the fat content, you can accommodate for many more carbohydrates.

Keep A Tab On Your Weekly Calorie Level

Whenever you are planning your diet intake or checking on your progress in terms of fat loss, be sure to assess your weekly intake of calories. This value must be with the range that allows optimal weight loss and is dependent on your body weight. In order to help you understand this concept better, let us take an example.

Let's assume that you consume 2,200 calories a day to maintain your body weight. This makes up 15,400 calories for the week. If you wish to lose one pound of body weight per week, you will need to create a calorie deficiency of 3,500 calories. In other words, the allowable calorie intake for the week must be reduced to 11,900 calories. This reduces your allowable daily intake to 1700 calories.

Let us take these numbers into the carb cycling perspective now. If you are planning to go on high carb for three days, then you will be looking to consume more than maintenance calories on these days. Assuming that you maintain a caloric intake of 2400, your total calorie intake for these three days will be 7200. Keeping the weekly intake constant to 11,900, you have 4700 calories left that you can accommodate in the remaining 4 days. This leaves you with 1200 calories a day on your low carb days.

Although, the number of calories indicates an extremely low carb intake on the low carb days, this will not be a problem for you after a high carb day. If you still feel that the 1,200 calorie mark is too low for you to manage, you can accordingly adjust the high carb days by reducing the number of high carb days or reducing the amount of calories you plan to consume on those days. This will automatically increase the allowable calorie intake on the low carb days.

Carb cycling is all about balance and you will have to do these calculations every now and then to keep your body on track. While you can choose the food you eat and the calories you consume on a daily basis, you will have to do this within the weekly limit of calories or you will lose out on your efforts.

Now that you have an idea about what carb cycling is, how it can benefit you and all the things that you need to remember before you get started, it is time to actually get on the task. The one thing that you need to know and remember about carb cycling is that it is an advanced dietary plan and thus, it will require more planning than basic or conventional dietary approaches. This may be time-consuming at first, but it will be worth all the effort.

Chapter 4: Getting Started With Carb Cycling

Carb cycling can be performed in many different ways. In fact, an individual performing carb cycling can vary the high carb and low carb cycles in several unique ways. The beauty of this dietary approach is that it can take a lot of fine-tuning and adjustments as you move forward with it.

Although the first level of variation is performed when you decide the training sessions and cycles of carb days that you plan to follow, many higher-level adjustments at the week-level can also be performed. For instance you can go on a low carb diet for the first 11 days and take a high carb break for 3 days that follow (12th, 13th and 14th day).

Besides this, you can also experiment with the amount of calories you consume on a daily basis, keeping the weekly limit intact. On a higher level, you may also change the weekly limit to see the level at which you can stretch your body to push itself for weight loss. On the basis of your goals, exercise routine and lifestyle, you can chalk out a plan for yourself to get started.

You need to understand at this stage that your tolerance levels, activity, and muscle mass will determine the right amount of carbs per day for you. Therefore, there is no perfect formula to determine this. You will need to experiment with the carb values to see which value works the best for you. You may choose a daily-changing or monthly-changing carb cycling approach depending on your body type and activity level. For instance, an individual who has average activity levels can do just fine with a monthly approach, while an athlete will require daily changes in carb cycling.

Carbohydrate Food Sources Recommended For You

Foods rich in fructose must be avoided at all costs. With that said, there is a long list of foods that can be included in your diet. As a rule, it is good to include foods that are rich in minerals, vitamins and fiber. A word of caution here is that you must not treat high carb days as opportunities to splurge on all the high-calorie desserts and ruin all of your efforts. Therefore, making healthier choices is extremely important. Some of the foods that can easily be added your diet include:

- Whole Grains
  Grains that have not ben modified are known to have several health benefits, apart from being a perfect inclusion for your carb cycling diet plan. Some useful sources of whole grains include oats, rice and quinoa.

- Vegetables
  The mineral and vitamin content associated with each vegetable is different. Moreover, the color balance given by the inclusion of different vegetables also adds color high nutritive value to the food.

- Unprocessed Fruits

As is the case with vegetables, fruits also have different abilities and benefits. For instance, berries have anti-oxidant benefits without putting any glycemic load on the body.

- Legumes
  It is always a good idea to include carbohydrates that take longer to digest because they reduce hunger and curb cravings. In addition, foods that are rich in fiber and minerals are also beneficial. A food type that includes the benefits of both of these types of foods is a legume.

- Tubers
  One of the richest sources of carbohydrates are tubers like sweet potatoes and potatoes. When on a high carb day, it is a good idea to pick them for a quick increase in carbs.

Creating a Meal Plan for Carb Cycling

Although carb cycling is a good middle path as it does not restrict your carb intake completely and it lets you take a few high carb dishes, it doesn't mean that you can feast on pasta every alternate day. Moreover, carb cycling is recommended not just for people who are willing to lose weight, it is a recommended dietary strategy for people who are willing to build muscle.

One of the fundamental things about eating healthy carbs every now and then is that it keeps your metabolism steady. Moreover, the addition of vegetables and proteins to your regular diet in proportionate quantities keeps the insulin levels low enough so as to ensure that you lose weight and not lose muscle.

Carb cycling can be changed and altered to fit into your routine. However, if you are still unsure about where to start, here are a few things that you can consider and implement for putting together a weekly carb cycling menu.

- Identify the Right Formula
  The ideal plan for carb cycling is to alternate high carb and low carb days for the six days of the week and reserve reward meals for the seventh day. With that said, you may have different health objectives and personal health. Therefore, you will need to alter the carb cycling menu according to these factors. For example, if you wish to lose weight, you can be on five low carb days and follow it with two high carb days.

  On the contrary, if you wish to add weight and build muscle mass, you can have around five high carb days and follow them with two low carb days. However, if you put yourself on this regime, remember not to put all the high carb days together. In fact, alternate them with low carb days and space out all kinds of days across the landscape of the week.

- Choose Your Foods Wisely
  The carb cycling approach may sound to many as if it is okay to be on meat for the low carb days and indulge in your favorite pasta for the rest of the

week. This is not true at all. When you are on a high carb day, you can derive a majority of the calories from whole grains like legumes and fruits. They will play an instrumental role in keeping your energy levels high without letting you compromise on your weight loss goals.

The low carbs days are usually the toughest to decide on meals. Therefore, it is recommended that you derive your protein intake from eggs, tofu and lean meats during this period. You can choose any vegetable to complement the protein. Try to distance yourself from processed foods and keep your grocery shopping restricted to fresh staples.

- Eat the Right Snacks
  The idea behind carb cycling is not to starve and yet help you lose weight at the same time. It gives you the leverage to indulge in small snacks every now and then. If a bowl of sugary snack can help you remain on track, you are allowed to have it. The only condition is that you must have it on a high carb day.

- Make a Meal Plan
  Now that you have planned all the proteins and grains that you need to include in your diet, the next thing is to create a daily menu to follow. The typical calorie intake for men should be around 1500 calories a day while the same for a woman should not exceed 1200 calories.

Keeping this in view, it is also equally important to remember that this value varies from individual to individual. It is good to maintain this calorie count on a daily basis. Moreover, it is equally important to maintain the macronutrient constitution of the food you eat.

You can contact a dietician or use any of online calculators available to count the macronutrient constitution required per body weight to lose weight or gain mass. Another piece of advice for you is that you must eat your breakfast as early as possible after waking up. The rest of the allocated calories for the day can be spread out to four to six comparatively smaller meals.

Typical Meal Plans

A day can be divided into five meals: breakfast, morning snack, lunch, evening snack and dinner. For a low carb day, you can have 2 eggs for breakfast, a berry protein shake for the morning snack and oatmeal for the evening snack. The lunch can include grilled chicken with asparagus while the dinner can be steak with vegetables.

On the other hand, on a high carb day, oatmeal with fruits can be your breakfast, followed by a fruit like apples along with almond butter or honey as a morning snack. A turkey sandwich or burger for lunch and salad for the evening snack will make a good high carb combination. Your high carb day can end with grilled chicken and pasta.

The next three chapters include recipes that can be used to create a daily menu for your carb cycling plan. On the basis of your personal preferences and availability of ingredients, you can pick and try all of the recipes

.

Chapter 5: Breakfast Recipes

The day starts with the breakfast and this meal is just as important for the body as it is for your empty stomach. It is a known fact that eating healthy recipes early in the morning can impact health substantially. In view of this fact, this chapter presents a few carb cycling recipes that you can include in your breakfast to give a healthy start to your day.

Recipe #1: High Protein/ Low-Carb Strawberry Smoothie

Serves – 1

Ingredients –

- 1 cup ice cubes
- 1/2 cup nonfat milk
- 1 cup whole strawberries (frozen or fresh)
- 1.5 tablespoons Ground Flax
- 1.25 scoops of Whey protein

Instructions –

- Take the blender
- Put all the ingredients in the blender and blend until a smooth mixture forms.
- Instead of using ice, you may also use frozen strawberries.

Recipe #2: Turkey Cutlets

Serves – 4

Ingredients –

- 1 Large Egg
- 3/4 Cup Wheat Germ
- 1 lb. Turkey Cutlets
- 1/4 Cup Low-Fat Parmesan Cheese (Grated)

Instructions –

- Preheat oven to 400 degrees Fahrenheit.
- Flatten the cutlets by pounding them.
- Take a shallow bowl and using some water, scramble the egg.
- Take a large plate and mix the Parmesan and wheat germ in it.
- Now, take each of the cutlets, one-by-one, soak them the egg mixture and roll them over in the Parmesan and wheat germ mix.
- Place the cutlets on a cooling rack prepared for baking. In order to prepare the rack for baking, you must place a cookie sheet on the rack.
- Bake the cutlets for around 15 minutes. Remember to flip the cutlets when the timer clicks 7-8 minutes. Also, check if there is any pink area on the cutlet. Pink areas indicate that the cutlet is not done yet. Put them back in the oven for some more time until they are completely cooked.
- Once done, serve them hot.

Recipe #3: Roasted Asparagus

Serves – 4

Ingredients –

- Cooking Spray
- 2 tablespoons olive oil
- 1 clove garlic
- 17 ½ ounces Asparagus (fresh)
- 1 tablespoon balsamic vinegar
- Black Pepper (to taste)
- Sea Salt (to taste)

Instructions –

- Preheat oven to 450 degrees Fahrenheit.
- Prepare the asparagus for cooking by removing the woody ends and washing it well.
- Now, take cloves, vinegar and oil and toss the asparagus in these ingredients. To finish, you must season the tossed asparagus with pepper and salt.
- Take a shallow baking dish and prepare it for baking by spraying some cooking spray over it.
- Lay the asparagus in the baking dish and allow it to cook for 6-10 minutes, until it is done.

Recipe #4: Breakfast Soufflé

Serves – 5

Ingredients –

- 5 bowls Mix Vegetables
- 20 Egg Whites
- Salt (to taste)
- Pepper (to taste)
- 1.25 cups Cheese (Shredded)
- Oil

Instructions –

- Take the egg whites and beat them until it becomes fluffy. Add salt and pepper, along with any other seasoning that you prefer.
- Take a shallow pan and put it on medium flame. Pour some oil and allow it to heat up. Sauté the vegetables until they are half done. You may also add meat or chicken pieces here, if you may like.
- Preheat the oven at 400 degrees Fahrenheit.
- Take a square baking pan and spray it well with cooking spray. Put the vegetables in the baking dish and bake for 20 minutes.
- Top the baked vegetables with shredded cheese and put the baking dish back into the oven. Bake until the cheese melts completely.
- Serve hot.

Recipe #5: Summer No-Cook Oatmeal

Serves – 1

Ingredients –

- 1/2 cup Milk
- 1/2 cup Oats
- 1 teaspoon Cinnamon
- Around 25 Raisins

Instructions –

- Place all the ingredients listed above in into a bowl.
- Cover the bowl and refrigerate it overnight.
- You can have this delicious oatmeal the next morning for breakfast.
- You may vary the amount of milk added to the oats for variety.

Recipe #6: Bacon and Egg Crumble

Serves – 1

Ingredients –

- 5 Egg Whites
- 2 Slices Turkey Bacon
- 1/4 cup Oatmeal
- 1 tablespoon Onion (dried)
- 1/4 teaspoon Black Pepper

Instructions –

- To prepare the turkey bacon for this recipe, you'll need to ensure that it is fully cooked.
- Mix in all the ingredients listed above into a microwavable bowl.
- Put the microwave on high and place the bowl in the microwave.
- Cook for 90 seconds.
- Take the bowl out and stir. Put the bowl back into the microwave and cook for another 90 seconds.
- You may also use Canadian bacon as a substitute of turkey bacon. Moreover, for variety you can add the vegetables of your choice to this dish.

Recipe #7: Peanut Butter Flax Hot Cereal

Serves – 1

Ingredients –

- ¼ teaspoon cinnamon
- 2 tablespoon peanut butter
- 1/2 cup boiling water
- 4 tablespoon flax meal

Instructions –

- Take the flax meal and pour water over it. Stir thoroughly.
- Add cinnamon and butter to this mixture.
- Allow the mixture to thicken by leaving it aside for around 2 minutes.

Recipe #8: Microwaved Banana

Serves – 1

Ingredients –

- 1 Medium Banana (ripened)
- 1 Large Egg
- Cooking Spray
- Optional:
    - Cocoa powder
    - Cardamom
    - Vanilla Extract
    - Cinnamon

Instructions –

- Spray a custard bowl with cooking spray.
- Break the egg and put it into the bowl. Whip well.
- Put the banana into this whipped egg and mash the banana well into the mixture.
- Add the optional flavors and microwave the mixture on full power for around 3 minutes.
- Serve!

Recipe 9: Pumpkin Muffins

This recipe makes 12 muffins.

Ingredients –

- ¼ cup Egg White
- ½ can Pumpkin (pure)
- 1 cup Sweetener (Splenda)
- ¼ teaspoon Nutmeg
- 1 cup Whole Wheat Flour
- ¼ teaspoon All Spice
- 6 tablespoons Apple sauce
- ¼ teaspoon Baking Powder
- ¼ teaspoon Cinnamon
- 1/8 teaspoon Ground Cloves
- ¼ teaspoon Baking Soda
- ¾ teaspoon Salt

Instructions –

- Preheat the oven to 350 degrees Fahrenheit.
- Take a bowl and add all the dry ingredients. Mix well.
- Take another bowl and mix all the wet ingredients in it.
- Now add the dry ingredients mixture to the wet ingredients mixture.
- Pour the batter into buttered muffin molds or a prepared baking dish.
- Bake for 30-35 minutes.

- You can increase the sweetness by adding another half cup of sweetener. Moreover, for variation, you may also add dark chocolate chips to the batter for added flavor.

Recipe #10: Deviled Eggs

Serves – 6

Ingredients –

- 1 teaspoon Hearty Deli Brown Mustard
- 2 tablespoons Mayo
- 1 teaspoon Sweet Pickles (finely chopped)
- 6 large Hard Boiled Egg
- Black Pepper (to taste)
- Salt (to taste)
- Paprika (for garnishing)

Instructions –

- This recipe requires hard-boiled eggs. So, boil the eggs for around 15 minutes before starting with the recipe.
- Once the eggs are done, peel the outer layer off and cut them into halves.
- Take the yolks out and put the hollow whites in a serving dish.
- Take a bowl and put all the removed yellows in it. Add all the other ingredients (except paprika) to this bowl and mix well.
- Put this mix into the hollows of the egg whites.
- Garnish with paprika and serve.

Chapter 6: Lunch/Dinner Recipes

Lunch and dinner are the two biggest and most filling meals of the day. As a result, we tend to eat much more during these meals as compared to shorter meals like evening tea and breakfast. Considering this, lunch/dinner form a crucial part of any diet plan. This chapter presents complete recipes to fill the carb cycling meal with healthy yet mouthwatering food.

Recipe #1: Clean Chicken, Veggies and Potato Bake

Serves – 4

Ingredients –

- 2 Skinless Chicken Breasts
- Cooking Spray
- 1/2 bunch asparagus
- 3 medium Red Potatoes
- 4 garlic gloves
- 1/3 cup fresh basil
- 1 teaspoon fresh rosemary
- Ground Pepper (to taste)
- 1.5 tablespoon Olive Oil
- Optional:
    - 1/2 cup Chicken Broth

Instructions –

- Before starting with the recipe, prepare the ingredients. Cut the chicken breast into small cubes, say 2-inch in size. Also, chop the potatoes, basil, garlic gloves and rosemary.
- Now, take the asparagus and trim it into smaller, 1-inch sized pieces. You can also take vegetables or peppers of your choice to add to this recipe.
- Preheat the oven to 400 degrees Fahrenheit.
- Take a baking dish and prepare it for baking by spraying it with cooking spray.
- Add potatoes, chicken, vegetables, tomatoes, garlic, basil, olive oil and chicken broth (if desired).
- Season it with pepper and sprinkle some rosemary on the top.
- Bake the dish for close to 45 minutes and serve.

Recipe #2: Grilled Peppers

Serves – 6

Ingredients –

- 2 tablespoon Extra Virgin Olive Oil
- 4 peppers
- 1/4 cup chopped parsley (fresh)
- 1/4 teaspoon Pepper
- 1/2 teaspoon Salt

Instructions –

- Set the grill on medium and preheat.
- You can use different colored peppers for this recipe. Prepare the peppers by cutting them length-wise and removing the seeds and stems.
- Take a Ziploc bag and add peppers, salt, pepper and oil in it. Shake the bag after sealing it well.
- Place the peppers on the grill. Ensure that the skin side is not facing the grill.
- Cover and allow the grill to cook on hot for 4-5 minutes. Flip the side of the peppers and allow it to cook for another 3-4 minutes.
- Take the peppers out of the grill and place them in a bowl.
- Add parsley and toss before serving.

Recipe #3: Veggie Kebabs

Serves – 8

Ingredients –

- Marinade
  - 3 tablespoons Olive Oil
  - 1 tablespoon Dijon mustard
  - 2 tablespoons Lemon Juice
  - 1 tablespoon Fresh Parsley, chopped
  - 2 tablespoons Red Wine Vinegar
  - 1 tablespoon Fresh Basil, chopped
  - 2 clove garlic, minced
  - Pepper (to taste)
  - Salt (to taste)
- Veggies
  - 2 cups Mushrooms
  - 2 cups Zucchini
  - 2 cups Sweet onion

Instructions –

- Before starting the recipe, be sure to prepare the ingredients. For instance, chop the parsley and basil. Also, slice and half the zucchini, sweet onions and mushrooms. You can also add a lot of other vegetables.
- Take a bowl and mix all the ingredients of the marinade in it.
- Take a shallow pan and arrange all the vegetables in it in such a manner that you create a first layer.

- Put the marinade mix over the layer of vegetables and put the pan in the refrigerator, leaving it aside for 2-4 hours.
- Now, take 8 skewers and arrange the vegetables on these skewers. Barbeque and grill the vegetables for 10-15 minutes. Do not forget to brush the leftover marinade on the vegetables as they are cooking.
- Serve hot.

Recipe #4: Cauliflower Rice

Serves – 8

Ingredients –

- 1 cauliflower
- Margarine

Instructions –

- Chop the cauliflower finely so much so that they become the size of rice.
- Steam the cauliflower for 5 minutes or till the cauliflower is done.
- Add margarine to the cooked cauliflower and serve.

Recipe #5: Mashed Cauliflower With Herb and Flavor

Serves – 3

Ingredients –

- 3 wedges Light Herb and Garlic Cheese
- 1 medium Cauliflower
- 1 teaspoon black pepper

Instructions –

- Take the cauliflower and cook it in steam until it becomes soft.
- Take a bowl and mash the cauliflower in the bowl using a hand blender.
- Now, add the pepper and cheese.
- Mash again using the hand blender until the mashed mix reaches the desired consistency.
- Serve the dish hot.

Recipe #6: Zucchini and Squash

Serves – 6

Ingredients –

- 3-4 Garlic Cloves
- 3 tablespoons Olive Oil
- 2 cups Zucchini (sliced)
- 1 cup onion (chopped)
- 2 cups Yellow Squash (sliced)

Instructions –

- Before starting the recipe, mince the garlic cloves.
- Take a sauté pan and add olive oil to it.
- Once the oil heats up, add minced garlic and chopped onion. Fry the garlic and onion for a couple of minutes until the onion become transparent.
- Now, add squash and zucchini to the pan. Fry the vegetables until they become golden brown.
- Add some water, switch the stove off and cover the pan with a lid. Allow the ensemble to cook for 5 minutes.
- Serve hot.

Recipe #7: South Beach Vegetable Beef Soup

Serves – 9

Ingredients –

- 1/3 cup Barley (pearled)
- 1.5 cup Onions (chopped)
- 3 tablespoon Extra Virgin Olive Oil
- 1.75 cups Carrots (chopped)
- 8 cups Beef Broth
- 1 Garlic Clove
- ¾ cup Celery (diced)
- Chopped Stewing Beef

Instructions –

- Take a large stockpot. Put 2 tablespoons of olive oil in this pot and heat it.
- Add onions to the pot and fry until the onions become golden brown.
- To the pot, add carrots, beef stock, garlic and celery.
- Take a frying pan and fry brown beef in 1 tablespoon of olive oil.
- Put the fried brown beef and barley.
- Cook for around one hour until the barley becomes tender.
- Serve.

Recipe #8: Roast Pork with Garlic Pepper Crust

Serves – 4

Ingredients –

- 1 lb. Pork Tenderloin
- 1 teaspoon Dried Parsley Flakes
- 5 Garlic Cloves (minced)
- 1/2 teaspoon Dried Thyme Leaves
- 1 teaspoon Olive Oil
- 1 tablespoon Lemon Juice
- 1 teaspoon Pepper

Instructions –

- Preheat the oven to 450 degrees Fahrenheit.
- Take a shallow roasting pan and line the same with tin foil.
- Prepare the pan for roasting by spraying it with cooking spray.
- Take a small bowl and add thyme, parsley, pepper and garlic to it.
- Coat the pork tenderloins with lime juice. You can either use a brush or hand for this purpose.
- Now, rub the tenderloins with the pepper-garlic mix from the side and top.
- Place the tenderloins on the roasting pan in such a manner that the coated side of the tenderloins is the upper side.

- Bake the tenderloins for around 30 minutes at 450 degrees Fahrenheit. You will know that the tenderloins are done if the center of the tenderloins is no longer pink in color.
- Once done, allow the tenderloins to stand for 10 minutes.
- Cut diagonal pieces and serve.

Recipe #9: Turkey Meatloaf

Serves – 8

Ingredients –

- 20 oz. Ground Turkey
- 1 cup Brown Rice (cooked)
- 2 Eggs
- 1 cup Black Beans
- 1/2 Green Pepper
- 1 slice wheat bread
- 1/4 cup Onion

Instructions –

- Dice the green peppers.
- Toast the white bread and crumble it for the recipe.
- Take a big bowl and mix all the ingredients together.
- Take a 13x9 inch loaf pan. Pour the mixture into the pan and cook for around 1 hour.
- You will know it is done when the upper layer starts getting brown in color.

Recipe #10: Boneless BBQ Pork Strips

Serves – 4

Ingredients –

- Olive Oil Spray
- 1/4 cup + 2 tablespoons BBQ Sauce
- 1.25 lbs. boneless pork tenderloin
- Garlic Powder (to taste)
- Grounded Black Pepper (to taste)
- Sea Salt (to taste)

Instructions –

- Half the tenderloins length-wise into 8 strips.
- Coat the strips with garlic powder, pepper and salt.
- Take a plastic container of medium size and place the strips in it.
- Coat the strips with 1/4th cup of BBQ sauce. Refrigerate the strips overnight.
- Put the broiler on preheat and prepare it by putting a medium-sized non-stick aluminum sheet. Spray some cooking spray over this sheet.
- Take the strips out of the refrigerator and place them over this baking sheet. Ensure that you don't put them one over the other. They should form a single layer.
- Allow the strips to cook on broil for 2-3 minutes. Now, flip the strips and allow the other side to cook for another 2-3 minutes.

- Serve the strips hot. You can pour the extra sauce over them before serving.

Recipe #11: Turkey Spinach Burger

Serves – 6

Ingredients –

- 1/2 cup Parmesan Cheese
- 4 cloves of Garlic
- 1 package of Frozen Spinach
- 1 1/2 lb. lean Ground Turkey
- 2 tablespoons dried basil
- 2 tablespoons olive oil
- Pepper (to taste)
- Salt (to taste)

Instructions –

- Chop the garlic before starting.
- Take the frozen spinach and defrost it. Be sure to strain out any excess water.
- Take a large bowl and mix in olive oil, dried basil, cheese, spinach, garlic and ground turkey. Add salt and pepper on the basis of your taste and preferences.
- Form patties of this mixture.
- Take a pan and put it on medium heat. Cook the patties on the pan. Alternatively, you can also barbeque them on the grill.
- Place the patty between the burger bun along with burger sauce, onions and tomatoes to finish.

Recipe #12: Beef Meatballs

This recipe makes 12 meatballs.

Ingredients –

- 1 egg
- 1/2 cup onion (finely chopped)
- 1 1/2 lbs. Extra Lean Ground Beef
- 2 tablespoons fresh basil, finely chopped
- 2 garlic cloves (pressed)
- 2 tablespoons fresh parsley, finely chopped
- 1 cup breadcrumbs
- 2 tablespoons fresh oregano, finely chopped
- 1 teaspoon Black Pepper (freshly grounded)
- 1 teaspoon Sea Salt

Instructions –

- Beat the egg lightly.
- Preheat the oven to 400 degrees Fahrenheit.
- Take a large bowl. Put breadcrumbs and egg in this bowl. Also, add in the spices and mix well.
- Now, add in the other ingredients while mixing.
- Make meatballs using an ice-cream scoop.
- Take a cookie sheet and spray it with cooking spray. Put the meatballs on this cookie sheet.
- Bake for around 20 minutes and serve hot.

Recipe #13: Turkey Meatballs

This recipe makes 16 meatballs.

Ingredients –

- Olive Oil Spray
- 1/4 cup Milk (non-fat)
- 1 lb. Extra Lean Ground Turkey
- 1 teaspoon Rosemary (dried)
- 1 large Egg White
- 1/4 cup breadcrumbs
- 1 teaspoon Oregano (dried)
- 1/4 teaspoon Black Pepper (grounded)
- 1 teaspoon Thyme (dried)
- 1/2 teaspoon Sea Salt
- 1 teaspoon Basil (dried)

Instructions –

- Take a large bowl and add all the ingredients in the bowl. Mix well.
- Prepare a cookie sheet for baking by spraying it with olive oil spray.
- Prepare meatballs from the mix and place them on the prepared cookie sheet.
- Bake the meatballs for 12-15 minutes at 400 degrees Fahrenheit.
- Serve hot.

Recipe #14: Chicken Fajitas

Serves – 4

Ingredients –

- 1 cup Low-fat Shredded Cheddar Cheese
- 1 Vidalia Onion
- 2 Chicken Breast (boneless and skinless)
- 4 Whole Wheat Low-carb Tortillas
- 1 Green Bell Pepper
- 2 Tomatoes
- Marinade:
    - 1/2 teaspoon Black Pepper (grounded)
    - 2 Garlic cloves
    - 1 tablespoon Tabasco sauce
    - 1 teaspoon Paprika
    - 1 tablespoon Honey

Instructions –

- Cut the chicken breast, onions and green bell peppers into strips.
- Also, dice the tomatoes and mince the garlic cloves.
- Take a bowl and mix all the marinade ingredients. To this bowl, add the chicken strips and mix until all the strips are coated with the marinade. Allow the marinade to settle for 10 minutes.
- Take a large pan and heat olive oil in it. Fry the chicken and put it in a plate.
- Now, stir-fry the peppers and onions until they are done. Add to this, the chicken and mix well.

- Take a low-carb tortilla and roll up $1/4^{th}$ of the mixture along with died tomatoes and $1/4^{th}$ shredded cheese into it. Serve!

Recipe #15: Chicken Strips

Serves – 2

Ingredients –

- 2/3 cup Panko Breadcrumbs
- 1/2 pound Chicken Strips (boneless and skinless)
- 1/2 teaspoon Black Pepper
- 1 Egg Whites
- Salt (to taste)
- 1/4 teaspoon Cayenne Pepper

Instructions –

- Beat the eggs well.
- Preheat the oven to 400 degrees Fahrenheit.
- Take a shallow bowl. Add the breadcrumbs along with the seasonings.
- Put the chicken strips into the egg white and then roll it up in the breadcrumbs mix.
- Take a baking sheet and spray some cooking spray over it.
- Put the strips on the baking sheet and cook for around 30 minutes. Remember to flip the side after around 15 minutes have passed.

Recipe #16: Taco Seasoning

Serves: 1

Ingredients –

- 1 tablespoon Flour
- 1 tablespoon Chili Powder
- 1/4 teaspoon Oregano
- 1/4 teaspoon Garlic Powder
- 1/2 teaspoon Paprika
- 1/4 teaspoon Onion Powder
- 1.5 teaspoon Cumin
- 1/4 teaspoon Red Pepper (crushed)
- 3/4 teaspoon Black Pepper
- 1/4 teaspoon Salt

Instructions –

- Take a bowl and mix all the spices in it.
- Take browned meat and add the spices to it along with ½ cup water. Cook until most of the liquid dries up.

Recipe #17: Broccoli for Everyone

Serves: 2

Ingredients –

- 1 tablespoon Olive Oil
- 2 Garlic Cloves
- 1 lemon
- 1 crown Broccoli (fresh)
- Salt (to taste)
- Black Pepper (to taste)

Instructions –

- Mince the garlic cloves. Chop the broccoli.
- Take a large sauté pan and heat olive oil in it over medium heat.
- To this, add garlic and fry until it turns golden brown.
- Add lemon zest and broccoli to the sauté pan. Cover with a lid and allow the broccoli to cook until it becomes tender.
- Stir in lemon juice and mix well.
- Add seasonings like salt and pepper.

Recipe #18: Garlic-Flavored Roasted Asparagus

Serves – 2

Ingredients –

- 1 tablespoon Olive Oil
- Red Pepper Flakes (crushed)
- 16 medium Asparagus spears
- Black Pepper (grounded)
- 3 Garlic cloves

Instructions –

- Slice the garlic cloves finely.
- Trim the asparagus spears.
- Preheat the oven to 400 degrees Fahrenheit.
- Take a large baking dish. Put the asparagus into the dish along with garlic and olive oil. Add red pepper flakes and black pepper to it. Mix well.
- Cook the asparagus for around 15 minutes or until the asparagus becomes tender.
- Serve hot.

Recipe #19: Dairy-free Protein Powder Pancakes

This recipe makes 4 pancakes.

Ingredients –

- 1 scoop Low-carb Protein Powder
- 1/2 cup Hot Water
- 1/2 cup Quaker Oats
- 1/4 teaspoon Ground Cinnamon
- 1/4 cup Egg Whites
- Optional:
  - Almond Extract
  - Blueberries
  - Almond butter

Instructions –

- Take a bowl and mix oats with hot water in it. Allow it to stand for a few minutes undisturbed.
- In another bowl, break the eggs and add protein powder to it.
- Now, stir in the oats to this mix.
- Stir in all the other ingredients to make a batter.
- Take a frying pan and spray some cooking spray on it.
- Make pancakes using the batter and serve hot.

Recipe #20: Baked Buffalo Chicken Nuggets

Serves – 2

Ingredients –

- 8 ounces chicken (boneless and skinless)
- 1/3 cup Whole-wheat Breadcrumbs
- 1 teaspoon Garlic Powder
- 1 teaspoon Cayenne Pepper
- 1 teaspoon Onion Powder
- 2 tablespoons Hot Sauce
- 1 teaspoon Black Pepper

Instructions –

- Cut the chicken into chunks, bite-sized.
- Preheat the oven to 375 degrees Fahrenheit.
- Take a shallow dish and mix in onion powder, breadcrumbs, cayenne pepper, garlic powder and black pepper.
- Take another shallow dish and add the chicken along with hot sauce in it. Mix well in such a way that hot sauce coats the chicken pieces completely.
- Now, roll the chicken into the breadcrumbs mix.
- Take a baking sheet and spray some cooking spray on it.
- Place the chicken pieces on the baking sheet and cook for around 10 minutes.
- Turn the pieces around and cook for another 8-10 minutes.
- Serve the chicken with hot sauce and celery.

Recipe #21: Oven-fried Parmesan Chicken

Serves – 4

Ingredients –

- 4 Chicken Breasts (boneless and skinless)
- 3 tablespoons Parmesan Cheese
- 1 teaspoon dried Thyme
- 1 Egg White
- 1/4 teaspoon Black Pepper and Salt
- 1.5 cups Cornflakes, crushed

Instructions –

- Preheat the oven to 400 degrees Fahrenheit.
- Take a bowl and beat the egg in it till the time the egg becomes fluffy.
- Take another bowl and add thyme, pepper, salt, cornflakes and cheese in it.
- Take every chicken piece one at a time and put it in the egg mixture followed by a roll-up in the cornflakes mix.
- Take a baking pan and spray it with cooking spray. Put the chicken breasts on the baking pan and cook for around 30 minutes.
- Serve hot.

Recipe #22: Fried Chicken

Serves – 4

Ingredients –

- 1 cup Panko breadcrumbs (Japanese style)
- 4 Chicken Breasts (boneless and skinless)
- 1/2 cup Liquid Egg Substitute
- 1/3 cup Whole Wheat Flour
- Black Pepper (to taste)
- Sea Salt (to taste)

Instructions –

- Preheat the oven to 425 degrees Fahrenheit.
- Take a zip lock bag and add flour and seasoning to the bag.
- Take another zip lock bag and put breadcrumbs into it.
- Take a bowl and add egg substitute to it.
- Put the chicken in the seasoning Ziploc bag. Toss until the chicken is completely coated.
- Now, coat the chicken with egg substitute and finally, roll it up in the breadcrumbs.
- Take a broiler pan and put the chicken in it.
- Allow the chicken to cook for 25 minutes at 425 degrees Fahrenheit.
- Remove and serve hot.

Recipe #23: Chicken Hot Wings

Serves – 2

Ingredients –

- 8 ounces Chicken Breast (boneless and skinless)
- 1 teaspoon Onion Powder
- 1 teaspoon Black Pepper
- 1 teaspoon Garlic Powder
- 1 teaspoon Cayenne Pepper
- 6 teaspoon Tabasco Sauce
- 1 cup Breadcrumbs

Instructions –

- Cut the chicken breasts into nugget-sized pieces.
- Preheat the oven to at 375 degrees Fahrenheit.
- Take a dish and put breadcrumbs to it. Put seasonings to this bowl and mix.
- Take another dish and put chicken pieces in it. Put hot sauce in this dish and mix in such a manner that the chicken pieces get coated with hot sauce. Cover the dish with a lid and leave it.
- Take a baking pan and prepare it for baking by spraying it with cooking spray.
- Now take each of the chicken pieces and roll it in breadcrumbs.
- Put these chicken pieces in the baking dish and bake for around 10 minutes.
- Change the side of the chicken pieces and bake for another 10 minutes.

- Serve hot.

Recipe #24: Chicken Noodle Soup

Serves – 12

Ingredients –

- Stock:
    - 2 stalks Celery
    - 1 teaspoon Black Peppercorns
    - 1 Onion
    - 3 pound Whole Chicken
    - 2 Carrots
    - 1 Bay Leaf
    - 1 gallon Cold Water
- Soup:
    - 2 stalks Celery
    - 2 Carrots
    - 1 tablespoon Olive Oil
    - 1 Onion
    - 1 teaspoon dried Thyme
    - 4 ounces Whole Wheat Pasta
    - 1 teaspoon dried Basil
    - 1/2 teaspoon dried Oregano
    - Black Pepper (to taste)
    - Salt (to taste)

Instructions –

- Chop the onions and dice the celery and carrots for the stock.
- For the soup, cut the carrots into strips and dice the onions and celery.
- Remove the chicken's skin.

- Take a stockpot and put the chicken in the pot. Also, add the cold water to the pot.
- Add the carrots, onion and celery to the pot along with peppercorns and bay leaf.
- Allow the mix to come to a boil and cook it on simmer heat. Now, let the stock cook for at least 45 minutes.
- Once done, strain the stock using a strainer.
- Take 1/4th of the stock and put it in the freezer. Use the remaining stock for soup.
- Take a stockpot and put oil in it. Add in the vegetables and let it cook for 5-8 minutes. Add the vegetables meant for soup to the stockpot. While the vegetables are cooking, remove the flesh from the chicken bones.
- To the soup, add the pasta, chicken flesh and seasonings to the soup.
- Allow the soup to cook for another 10 minutes and serve hot.

Recipe #25: Baked Chicken with Garlic and Sun-dried Tomatoes

Serves – 4

Ingredients –

- Black Pepper (to taste)
- 1 tablespoon Olive Oil
- 1 pound Boneless Chicken Breasts
- 1 medium Onion
- 20 Garlic cloves
- 1/4 cup White Wine
- 1/2 cup sun-dried Tomatoes
- 1 teaspoon dried Oregano
- 1/2-3/4 cup Chicken Stock

Instructions –

- Cut the chicken breast into smaller pieces.
- Peel the garlic cloves and slice the onion into thin pieces.
- Chop the tomatoes to smaller pieces.
- Preheat the oven to 325 degrees Fahrenheit.
- Wash the chicken with cold water and rinse.
- Take two garlic cloves and crush them nicely.
- Take an oven-safe skillet and place it over medium heat. Add oil to the pan.
- Add crushed garlic to the skillet and fry.
- On top of the crushed garlic, add chicken to the skillet. Add the rest of the garlic cloves to the skillet.

- Allow the chicken to cook for around 8 minutes. Once the side is done, flip the chicken to cook the other side. Let the chicken cook for another 4 minutes.
- Once done, chicken can be removed from the skillet.
- Now add tomatoes and onions to the skillet and cook for around 5 minutes.
- The heat under the skillet can be reduced before adding wine.
- Take the chicken back to the skillet. Once the chicken is half-done, add the stock to the skillet.
- Add seasonings like oregano and black pepper to the soup.
- Cover the skillet and bake the ensemble for 30 minutes.
- Serve hot.

Recipe #26: Balsamic Brussels Sprout

Serves – 6

Ingredients –

- ¼ cup Coconut Oil
- 6 cups Brussels sprouts
- Black Pepper (to taste)
- 1 tablespoon thick Balsamic Vinegar
- Sea Salt (to taste)
- For tuna:
  - Crushed Almonds
  - 2 tablespoons Coconut Oil
  - 3 Tuna Steaks
  - Pepper (to taste)
  - Sea Salt (to taste)

Instructions –

- Trim and split the sprouts for this preparation.
- Take a saucepan and add coconut oil to it. Place the pan on medium heat.
- When the oil is completely melted, add the sprouts, pepper and salt.
- Mix well and fry for a couple of minutes.
- Next, cover the pan with a lid, put the stove on low heat and let the sprouts cook for around 15 minutes.
- To the pan, add balsamic vinegar and stir well. Again, cover the pan with a lid and cook for another 10 minutes. By now, the sprouts would have become tender.

- In order to prepare tuna to be served along with the brussel sprouts, take the food processor and crush some almonds in it.
- Take the tuna steaks and add salt and pepper to it. Coat these tuna steaks with the crushed almonds on all sides.
- Take a large frying pan and put coconut oil it. Allow the coconut oil to melt completely. Put the prepared tuna steaks in this pans and cook for a couple of minutes. Flip the side of the tuna steak and cook for another couple of minutes.
- Once both of the sides of the steak are done, remove the steak and slice it into strips.
- Serve the Brussels sprouts with tuna steaks.

Recipe #27: Zuppa Toscana

Serves – 2

Ingredients –

- 4 cups Water
- 2 cups Chicken Stock
- 3 cups chopped Kale
- 1 pound Italian Sausage
- 2 cloves Garlic
- 2 cups riced Cauliflower
- 1 tablespoon heavy Whipping Cream
- ½ cup diced onion
- ¼ cup Butter
- 1 teaspoon Red Pepper (crushed)
- Pepper (to taste)
- Salt (to taste)
- Optional:
  - Fresh-grated Parmesan

Instructions –

- Ground the Italian Sausage.
- Chop the garlic cloves.
- Take a large saucepan and add onion, sausage and garlic to it. Cook until they turn brown.
- Add some chicken stock to the pan to deglaze the pan.
- To the pan, also add salt, pepper, crushed red peppers and the remaining stock. Allow the ensemble to cook for half an hour.

- Add cauliflower, kale and butter and cook until the vegetables become tender. This should not take more than 15 minutes.
- Just when you are ready to serve or eat, add whipping cream and cheese.

Recipe #28: Low-Carb Beef and Broccoli Fry

Serves – 2

Ingredients –

- ¼ teaspoon Splenda
- 2 cups blanched Broccoli
- 1 tablespoon Canola Oil
- ½ cup Onion
- ½ cup Carrot (thinly sliced)
- 1½ tablespoons Chicken Broth
- 6 ounces boneless Sirloin Steak
- ½ teaspoon Cornstarch
- 1 tablespoon low-sodium Soy Sauce
- Optional:
    - ⅛ teaspoon Salt

Instructions –

- Cut the onion into wedges.
- Cut the sirloin steak into strips.
- Take a large skillet and add oil to it.
- Add onion, carrot and broccoli. Cook well until the vegetables become tender and crisp.
- Add beef and cook until it is done.
- Take a small bowl and stir in cornstarch, Splenda, chicken broth and salt.
- Add this mix to the vegetables and beef.
- Cook for around 2-3 minutes or until the sauce begins to thicken.
- Serve!

Recipe #29: Flank Steak Salad

Serves – 1

Ingredients –

- 12-ounce container small fresh mozzarella balls (marinated)
- 2 tablespoons Oregano Leaves (fresh)
- 1 large bunch Italian Parsley (fresh)
- ½ cup Olive Oil
- 3 Garlic cloves
- 1 teaspoon chipotle Hot Pepper Sauce
- ¼ cup Red Wine Vinegar
- 8 ounces mixed Baby Greens
- 1½ pounds Flank Steak

Instructions –

- Drain the fresh mozzarella balls.
- Before starting with the actual recipe, put the barbeque on medium heat so that it is prepared in time for the recipe.
- In a food processor, blend together garlic, oregano and parsley for around 10 seconds.
- To the blender, also add vinegar, ½ cup oil and hot pepper sauce. Blend well to form a smooth paste.
- Add salt and pepper to season.
- Prepare the grill rack by brushing it with oil.
- Add salt and pepper to the steaks and put it on grill.
- Remember to flip the side once one of the sides is done. It should take around 5 minutes per side.

- Once done, allow the steaks to rest for around 10 minutes.
- Take another bowl and add greens and some dressing to it.
- Take a platter and transfer the greens to it. Also, add mozzarella.
- Slice the steaks and add them to the greens.
- Put the rest of dressing on top of the ensemble.

Recipe #30: Wilted Greens and Seared Scallops

Serves – 1

Ingredients –

- 2 Shallots
- 12 large Sea Scallops
- 2 bunches of Kale
- 3 slices of Bacon (thickly-cut)
- 1 tablespoon Red Wine Vinegar
- 2 - 3 Garlic cloves
- 2 tablespoons Olive Oil
- Salt (to taste)
- 1 tablespoon Butter
- Pepper (to taste)
- 1 tablespoon Soy Sauce

Instructions –

- Cut the bacon into pieces.
- Thinly slice the shallots.
- Mince the garlic cloves.
- Cut large strips from kale leaves and cut the stem into small pieces.
- Take a high-sided pan and put it on medium-high heat.
- Put bacon pieces into the pan and allow the same to cook for around 3-4 minutes. To the pan, add shallots and cook again for 3-4 minutes. Stir in kale stems and garlic to the pan.

- Lastly, add kale leaves and cook until the leaves wilt.
- Season the bacon and kale mix with pepper, vinegar and soy sauce and remove from heat.
- Take a cast-iron skillet and place it over high heat. Add olive oil to it.
- Set the scallops aside and coat it with pepper and salt.
- By this time, the oil in the pan would have heated up. So, add scallops to the pan and allow them to cook for a couple of minutes.
- Flip the side of the scallops. To the cooking scallops, add butter and cook for another couple of minutes.
- Put these scallops over the bacon and kale mix and serve.

Recipe #31: Fried Eggs with Asparagus and Prosciutto

Serves – 4

Ingredients –

- 1 tablespoon flat-leaf parsley (coarsely chopped)
- Black Pepper (freshly grounded)
- Salt
- 16 spears Asparagus
- 4 large Eggs
- 1 tablespoon Butter (unsalted)
- 2 tablespoons Parmesan cheese (freshly grated)
- ¼ pound Prosciutto

Instructions –

- Melt the butter and slice the prosciutto thinly.
- Prepare the asparagus for cooking by removing tough ends.
- Take a large sauté pan and water along with some salt to it. Allow this salted water to come to a boil.
- Add asparagus to the pan and allow the asparagus to cook until it becomes tender. This should not take longer than 4-5 minutes.
- Rinse the asparagus of any excess water and fold it into a kitchen towel.
- Take a non-stick skillet and place it over medium-low heat. Add half of the butter mentioned in the ingredients list to the pan. Break an egg into the pan and cover the pan. Cook the egg for around 4 minutes or until the eggs are set. Don't forget to add

some salt and pepper to the eggs after breaking. Repeat this process for 4 eggs.

- Take four plates and place some prosciutto slices on them. Also add spears of asparagus to each of the plates. Spray some butter over the arrangement.
- Now, carefully, put the fried eggs in these plates and garnish the same with parsley and Parmesan cheese.

Recipe #32: Asian Chicken Salad

Serves –1

Ingredients –

- ½ bag of Slaw Mix
- 2 bags Carrots (shredded)
- 2 tablespoons Black Sesame Seeds
- ½ bag Kale (shredded)
- Meat from 1 rotisserie chicken
- 1 jalapeño
- 4 tablespoons Soy Sauce
- 2 limes
- 5 to 6 drops Honey
- 1 tablespoon Sriracha

Instructions –

- Halve the jalapenos and slice them finely.
- Shred the meat and squeeze out the juice from the 2 limes.
- Add all the ingredients to a re-sealable container.
- Shake well to mix and serve.

Recipe #33: Low - Carb Gourmet

Serves – 10

Ingredients –

- ½ cup low-fat Cream Cheese
- 1 large Head Cauliflower
- 1/2 cup fat-free Sour Cream
- 1 tablespoon Butter
- 1/4 cup Parmesan Cheese (freshly grated)
- 1/4 cup Green Onions (minced)
- 1 cup Cheddar Cheese
- 5 slices bacon

Instructions –

- Cook the bacon and crumble it well.
- Preheat the oven to 350 degrees Fahrenheit.
- Take the cauliflower and after removing the core and stem, cut the vegetable into smaller pieces.
- Take a large pot and add the cauliflower pieces along with enough water to cover the pieces. Cook the cauliflower until it becomes tender.
- Remove the cauliflower pieces and drain out all the water.
- Now, take a potato masher and mash the potatoes.
- Add cheese, 3/4th of the bacon, butter, cream cheese and sour cream to the mashed cauliflower.
- Take a casserole dish and spread the mashed mix in it. Add the rest of the bacon and cheese to the dish.

- Bake the dish for around 30 minutes or until the cheese becomes bubbly.
- Serve hot

Recipe #34: Quick Chicken Satay

Serves – 2

Ingredients –

- 1.5 tablespoon Soy Sauce
- 8 oz. Chicken Breast
- 1.5 tablespoon Natural Peanut Butter
- 1.5 tablespoon Water
- 1 teaspoon Garlic Powder
- 1 teaspoon Cayenne Pepper (or to taste)
- 1/2 cup Mushrooms
- 2 cup Green Beans

Instructions –

- Remove the skin from the chicken breasts and cut them into smaller pieces.
- Take a skillet (non-stick) and place it over medium heat. Add the chicken pieces and cook them until they are done.
- Take a steamer and place mushrooms and beans in it. Cook these vegetables until they become tender.
- Take a microwavable container and add garlic, cayenne, peanut butter, water and soy sauce in it. Microwave this mixture for around 45 seconds. Stir well to get a smooth mixture.
- Add the sauce to the chicken cubes and mix until the chicken cubes are well coated with the sauce.
- Serve the chicken with beans and mushrooms. Don't forget to add a dash of soy sauce for added effect and flavor.

Recipe #35: Grilled Caribbean Chicken

Serves – 4

Ingredients –

- 4 Chicken Breasts Halves (boneless and skinless)
- 1 teaspoon grated Orange Zest
- 1/4 cup Orange Juice (freshly squeezed)
- 1 tablespoon Extra-Virgin Olive Oil
- 1 tablespoon Lime Juice (freshly squeezed)
- 1 clove Garlic
- 1 teaspoon Grated Ginger
- 1/2 teaspoon dried and crushed Oregano
- 1/4 teaspoon Hot Pepper Sauce
- 1/4 teaspoon coarsely Ground Black Pepper
- 1/2 teaspoon coarse Kosher Salt

Instructions –

- Mince the garlic cloves.
- Take a shallow bowl and add orange zest, olive oil, lime juice, orange juice, garlic, ginger, oregano and hot pepper sauce to it.
- Now, add chicken to this mixture in such a manner that the chicken gets completely coated with this marinade.
- Allow the chicken to sit in the marinade for around 3 hours.
- Once the marinating time is over, remove the chicken and add pepper and salt to it.

- Place the chicken on the barbeque grill and remove when done.
- Serve hot.

Recipe #36: Eggplant Pizzettes

Serves – 2

Ingredients –

- 4 tablespoons Prego Spaghetti Sauce
- 4 slices of peeled Eggplant (fresh)
- 2 large Black Olives
- ¼ cup Mozzarella Cheese
- Black Pepper (to taste)
- Salt (to taste)

Instructions –

- Preheat the oven to 425 degrees Fahrenheit.
- Add salt and black pepper to the eggplant slices.
- Take a baking sheet and place the eggplant slices on it. Bake the dish for 6-8 minutes or until the eggplants are browned. During this time, remember to turn the side of the eggplant slices once.
- Take the eggplant slices out. Add pasta sauce and shredded cheese along with black olives to the eggplant slices.
- Bake these eggplant slices for around 3-5 minutes.

Recipe #37: Chicken and Green Bean Casserole

Serves – 4

Ingredients –

- 1 cup frozen Green Beans
- 1 lb. Chicken Breast
- 1/4 cup Cheddar Cheese
- 1 can (10.75 oz.) Cream of Chicken Soup

Instructions –

- Put the oven on preheat to 350 degrees Fahrenheit.
- Take the chicken breast and cut it into smaller pieces. Add seasoning to the pieces and coat them well with the seasoning.
- Take a skillet frying pan and fry the chicken pieces until they turn brown.
- Take a casserole dish and add soup and beans to it.
- Add the green bean mixture and chicken to this soup.
- To the mix, add water and add cheddar cheese.
- Allow the soup to bake for 20 minutes and serve hot.

Recipe #38: Cabbage and Sausage Soup

Serves – 8

Ingredients –

- 4 Cups Chopped Cabbage
- 1 lb. Louis Rich Turkey Smoked Sausage
- 1/2 cup Green Pepper (chopped)
- 1.5 Cups Sliced Zucchini
- 1 medium Onion (chopped)
- 1/2 cup Yellow Pepper (chopped)
- 1 can Stewed Tomatoes
- 2 cups Tomato juice
- 2 tablespoons Chili Powder
- 1 can Campbell's Tomato Soup
- 1 Celery stalk (chopped)
- 1/2 tablespoons Black Pepper
- 1/2 cup Chicken Broth
- 1/2 cup fresh Mushrooms (sliced)

Instructions –

- Take a stockpot and put broth in it. Add in the peppers, celery and onion to it. All the vegetables to cook and turn the heat off once they become tender.
- Take a large crockpot and put all the ingredients listed above in it.
- Cook the soup ingredients for 3 to 4 hours.
- Whenever the soup seems to have dried up, you can add tomato juice or water to it.
- Serve hot.

Recipe #39: Tomato and Mozzarella Salad

Serves – 1

Ingredients –

- 4 Red Ripe Tomatoes
- 1/8 cup Mozzarella Cheese
- 5 Garlic cloves
- 5 tablespoons Extra Virgin Olive Oil
- 5 tablespoons Fresh Basil
- 1 cup Mixed greens (salad)

Instructions –

- Cut the cheese into cubes and tomatoes into halves.
- Finely dice the garlic and basil.
- Take a bowl and add all the ingredients to the bowl.
- Toss nicely and serve.

Recipe #40: Faux Shepard's Pie

Serves – 8

Ingredients –

- 1/2 Onion
- 1 lb. Ground Beef
- ½ cup Cream Cheese
- 1 packet (10 oz.) Frozen Cauliflower
- 1 cup shredded Cheddar Cheese
- 1/4 + 2 tablespoons Heavy Cream
- Black Pepper (to taste)
- Salt (to taste)

Instructions –

- Take a frying pan and add some oil to it. To this, add onions and fry until onion become golden brown.
- Add ground beef also and cook until it is done. You will know that it is done once there is no visible pink area on the beef.
- Take a pie dish and spread the ground beef on it.
- On a hamburger, pour ¼ cup cream. Season the hamburger with salt and black pepper.
- Defrost the cauliflower and rinse well. Cook cauliflower until it becomes soft.
- Remove the cauliflower from heat and add 2 tablespoons of heavy cream and cream cheese.

- Blend the mix until all the ingredients are completely mashed and a potato mash – type mixture is obtained.
- To this mixture, add black pepper and salt.
- This cauliflower mixture must be poured over ground beef.
- On top of this, add cheddar cheese and bake the ensemble for 350 degrees Fahrenheit for 15 minutes or until the cheese completely melts.

Chapter 7: Dessert Recipes

Dessert is an essential and inseparable part of lunch and dinner in most cuisines. This makes it important for us to cover this section of food to give you a comprehensive list of recipes that can help you complete your daily plan in the manner that you like.

Recipe #1: Chocolate Smoothie Dessert

Serves – 3

Ingredients –

- 6.5 cups Ice Cubes
- 1.5 cups Cold Water
- 3 tablespoons Milk Powder (fat-free)
- 1/2 cup + 2 tablespoons Cocoa Powder (unsweetened)
- 12 packets Monk Fruit Powder
- 5 tablespoons Chocolate Pudding (sugar-free)

Instructions –

- Take the blender and add all the ingredients except ice cubes in the blender bowl.
- Blend well on medium for 30 seconds. Then, turn the blender speed to high and blend for another 30 seconds.
- Now, add ice cubes to the blender bowl, a few at a time. Blend well!

Recipe #2: Midnight Brownies

This recipe makes 8 brownies.

Ingredients –

- 1/4 cup Unsweetened Cocoa
- 1/2 cup Agave Syrup
- 1 can Black Beans
- 1/2 cup Egg Whites
- 6 tablespoons Chocolate Chips (Mini and Semi-sweet)
- 1/2 cup Self-Rising Flour
- 1 teaspoon Baking Powder
- 2 tablespoons Vanilla
- Cooking spray

Instructions –

- Preheat the oven to 350 degrees Fahrenheit.
- Take a baking dish (8x8) and spray it with cooking spray.
- Put all the ingredients, except the chips, in the food processor.
- Chop these ingredients until a fine consistency is achieved.
- Chop for another 20 seconds after cleaning the sides.
- Add in the chips and pour the batter into the baking dish.
- Bake the batter for around 20 minutes or until it is done.

- Allow the dish the cool down for an hour or so. Once the dish comes down to room temperature, scrap out the sides to remove the brownie cake from the baking dish.
- Cut the cake into brownies and serve.

Recipe #3: Dreamsicle Dessert

Serves – 6

Ingredients –

- 1 container (8 oz.) Cool Whip Free
- 1 box (1.4 oz.) S/F Fat Free Vanilla Instant Pudding
- 1 box (0.3 oz.) box S/F Orange Jell-O

Instructions –

- Prepare the Jell-O using the instructions specified on its box.
- Stir in the dry pudding mix and mix well.
- Add in the cool whip free and whisk the mixture.
- Now, pour the mixture into 6 individual cups and allow the mixture to refrigerate for a few hours.
- Serve, once done!

Recipe #4: Tofu Chocolate Cake

Serves – 16

Ingredients –

- 1 block (300 gm.) of soft/dessert tofu
- 1 box Chocolate Cake Mix
- 1/4 cup Water

Instructions –

- Take a large bowl and add the cake mix and tofu to it. Mix well using a hand mixer. You may also use a blender for this purpose.
- Once the mixture is nicely mixed, add water and blend well until a smooth consistency is achieved.
- Put the batter into a prepared baking dish and follow the instructions given on the cake mix box to prepare the cake. You may use cup cakes or a cake dish to make the cake. However, note that you do not have to add any egg or oil mentioned on the cake mix box because we have used tofu as its substitute.
- Once done, allow the cake to cool down to room temperature and serve.

Recipe #5: Low-fat/Sugar-free Blueberry Cheesecake

Serves – 8

Ingredients –

- 2 packets Cheesecake Pudding Mix (fat free, sugar-free)
- 1 container Whipped Dessert Topping (fat-free)
- 2 cups Blueberries
- 2 cups Non-fat Milk

Instructions –

- Take the pudding mix in a bowl and add in the milk. After mixing, you will get a thick mixture.
- Take a graham cracker shell and pour half of the pudding mix into this shell.
- Top the pudding with 1 cup of blueberries. You can alternatively use any other fruit as well. Slightly, press the fruit into the pudding.
- In the other half of the pudding, add the whipped topping. Put this mixture over the blueberries.
- On top of this layer, pour the remaining cream and blueberries.
- Allow this ensemble to refrigerate for a couple of hours.
- The dessert is ready to serve once it is set.

Recipe #6: Momritz Cinnamon Bread

Serves – 12

Ingredients –

- 3 cup Organic Bread Flour
- 1 large Egg
- 1/4 cup Unsalted Butter
- 1 cup Milk (non-fat)
- 1/2 teaspoon Salt
- 1/2 cup Sugar
- 2 teaspoon Baker's Yeast
- 1.5 tablespoon Grounded Cinnamon

Instructions –

- Take a bread machine and load all the ingredients listed above into it.
- Set the bread machine on the sweet or dough cycle.
- Slice the bread once done.
- In order to ensure that the crust remains soft, plastic wrap the bread as soon as you remove the bread out of the bread machine.

Recipe #7: Low-carb Chocolate Mousse

Serves – 6

Ingredients –

- 1 tub (8oz) Cool Whip Free Topping
- 2 cups Milk (fat-free)
- 1 packet Jell-O Chocolate Instant Pudding Mix

Instructions –

- Pour the milk into a bowl.
- Slowly add the pudding mix to the milk and mix well. You may use a hand-mixer for this purpose. Keep scraping the sides.
- Now, add in the topping and continue mixing.
- Take 6 dessert dishes and pour the mixture into them.

Recipe #8: Prairie Harpy's Mega Chocolate Protein Fudge

Serves – 12

Ingredients –

- 1.5 cups Cheese (at room temperature)
- 2 squares Ghirardelli Chocolate (unsweetened)
- 4 tablespoons Salted Butter
- 3 scoops Lean Dessert Chocolate protein powder
- 1 teaspoon Stevita Delight Chocolate

Instructions –

- Take a saucepan and place it over low heat. Put the butter into this pan and allow it to melt.
- Now, add the chocolate to this pan and allow the same to melt as well.
- Just when the chocolate seems to be slightly melted, remove the pan from heat and stir until a smooth mixture of chocolate and butter is obtained.
- To this melted chocolate, add Stevita and mix well.
- Also, add in the protein powder and continue stirring until a fudgy mix is obtained.
- Take 12 bowls and fill them with the fudgy mix. Put them in the freezer overnight.
- You can remove one cup a day to eat it. Let the other cups remain in the freezer. This will help you regulate your intake as well.

Recipe #9: Lite Shortcake

Serves – 6

Ingredients –

- 6 Dessert Shells
- ½ cup Sugar
- 1 serving of Lite Cool Whip
- 4 cups Strawberries

Instructions –

- Take a large bowl and put all the strawberries into it. Put sugar over these strawberries. Set the bowl aside for 20 minutes to let the sugar settle into the berries.
- Take a potato masher and mash the strawberries.
- Put the strawberries mash into the dessert shells, taking one dessert cup at a time. Now, top the mashed strawberries with lite cool whip.

Recipe #10: Zero Carb Deep Chocolate Coconut Candy

This recipe makes 12 candies.

Ingredients –

- 3 tablespoons Cocoa Powder (unsweetened)
- 5 tablespoons Coconut Oil
- 3 drops liquid Sugar-free Sweetener
- 1/3 cup Unsweetened Coconut (shredded)

Instructions –

- Take a small saucepan and add coconut oil, sweetener and cocoa powder to the pan. Allow the coconut oil to melt completely. Mix until the cocoa powdered nicely mixed.
- Now, add shredded coconut to the pan.
- Take candy molds and pour the mixture into them.
- Put the molds into the refrigerator and leave them there for half an hour. If the chocolate doesn't seem to have become solid in this time, let the colds remain inside the refrigerator for a little longer.
- Once done, you can remove the candies from the molds and store them in a cool place in an airtight container.

Chapter 8: How to Make Carb Cycling Work For You

If you have followed any diet plan in the past then you know that diet plans can't often be considered a life-plan for you. Your body keeps changing and so does it's needs and diet plan required. Whenever you compel your body to follow a diet plan, it reacts to it upfront, but as time passes, the body adapts to these changes and the reactions gradually subside.

In order to allow your body to make the progress as expected, it is important to make necessary changes to the diet plan as and when required. It is estimated that most people show best results in the first couple of weeks of them following a diet plan. For instance, if someone is 200 pounds, then a loss of 4-8 pounds is expected. However, for someone who weighs lesser than 200 pounds, a loss of 2-5 pounds can be expected. For many people, a lot of this weight loss is water or so called water weight.

This number reduces for the subsequent weeks to about 0.5-1.5 pounds in a week if the individual weighs less than 200 pounds. However, for someone that weighs more than 200 pounds, weight loss of 1-3 pounds per week is normal. These numbers have been mentioned here to help you analyze if you are making normal progress with your current diet plan. If you unable to hit the lower range of these values, you can be sure that your diet plan needs some serious adjustment.

Adjusting The Carb Cycling Diet

In order to see progress on a weekly basis and remain on track, a good balance between cardio workouts and diet is required. In the carb cycling context, you can adjust the amount of carbohydrates you consume in your diet for the week by changing one high day to a low day. Consequently, this will increase the amount of fat you burn in that week.

In addition, you may also increase the number of days you perform cardio workouts for the week. If increasing the number of days doesn't sound feasible, you may also think about increasing the time that you spend for each session. In other words, if you started your carb cycling diet plan with 2 high carb days, 3 low carb days and 2 medium carb days, you can simply change it to 3 medium carb days, 1 high carb day and 3 low carb days. This will reduce your carbohydrate intake immediately. In addition, on the newly added medium carb day, you can also add a session of cardio.

As a rule, you can put your cardio sessions on all days when you are following a medium carb or low carb diet. You can skip the cardio on a high carb day. Increasing the duration of the cardio can also be a lot of help. For instance, you can simply add 10 minutes to each cardio session. This will add 40 minutes to your cardio workouts for the week if you are working out 4 days a week. This should help in keeping the weight loss on track.

It is important to mention here that people who have a slow metabolism can completely skip the high carb day and follow an all-medium and low carb day plan. As a consequence of this, they will be doing cardio everyday. If you hit a plateau, then you can even switch to an all-low carb day plan. This will put you on a very low carb diet.

Forcing your body to push too hard can shut down metabolism completely. As a consequence, you will not be able to advance with your weight loss plans. Therefore, it is better to take baby steps and start small. You can gradually take your body to a point where you push it hard enough to get the results you desire. It is recommended that you start with an easy diet and as you see your weekly progress chart improve, you can make necessary changes and modifications.

Keep A Check On Your Hormone Levels

Before concluding this chapter, a mention of how the hormones impact progress in weight loss is significant. Some people continue to see only sub-optimal results even after putting in their best efforts. No matter how much they increase their cardio and reduce their carbohydrate intake, no substantial results can be seen. For such people, a comprehensive blood test is recommended. Most commonly, the thyroid levels need to be observed. Another hormone that needs a quick review for men is testosterone.

No matter how good your diet and exercise routine is, nothing will ever work if your hormone levels don't let them. In case any adverse results are observed in the reports, medication and therapy can help to bring the levels back on track. A hormone replacement therapy or medication that can maintain the correct levels can be accomplished under the supervision of a medical practitioner.

Additional Tips

Apart from all the technical things that you need to keep a tab on in order to make your carb cycling diet work for you, here are a few common things that you can also include in your lifestyle for make things easier.

- Prepare a grocery list and purchase everything all at once, on a weekly basis. This will not only help you save time, but it will also help you save money.

- Another thing that you can do when you go grocery shopping is buy in bulk. This will help you save money and you will not have to visit the grocery store as often.

- If you plan to have a smoothie early in the morning, then you can simply add all the ingredients and store the mix in an airtight container a day before needed. In the morning, all you need to do is blend the smoothie with ice and consume. This will help you save time and you will have your first meal of the day ready in just a few minutes.

- In line with the previous tip, you can likewise prepare many other meals once a week and consume them on a day-to-day basis. However, be sure to store the prepared meat and vegetables in airtight containers in the freezer. Take the meal out of the freezer a night before you wish to consume it and put it in the refrigerator. The meal will be defrosted and ready to eat. Although, this may sound like a lot of hard work at first, you will get used to it in due time.

Conclusion

Carb cycling is a useful tool that has the capability to play an instrumental role in improving health, increasing performance and optimizing the diet in such a manner that you can lose weight and maintain a healthy lifestyle at the same time. Research has proven the multi-faceted benefits of carb cycling, short-term as well as long-term.

The fundamental idea behind the carb cycling dietary approach is to alternate low carb days and high carb days in such a manner that you aren't depleted of your energy and yet lose weight by controlling your calorie intake on a daily and weekly basis. The fact that it doesn't limit you benefits you psychologically, apart from the usual physical benefits that this regime has for your body.

The most important facet of this dietary approach is that it is not a static approach. You need to play around with the number of calories and high/low carb days to adjust to your lifestyle and body needs. This book includes basics of the carb cycling approach and all the other information required to get started with carb cycling. The recipes included in this book can help you create a healthy and delectable daily menu for yourself, keeping carb cycling in close view.

You can take the knowledge included in this book forward by implementing this dietary approach in your life along with all the other advice that has been given. Remember to make the required changes and customize the approach to suit your body needs and environment. We hope you benefit from this approach and make the best out of all your efforts towards a happy and healthy living.

Made in the USA
Middletown, DE
26 January 2019